Quilting Possibilities

Freehand Filler Patterns

Sue Patten

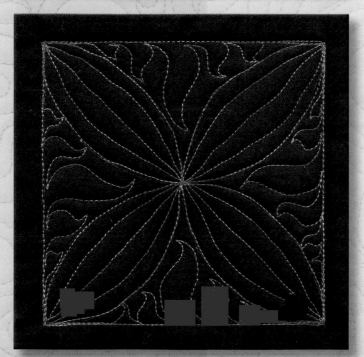

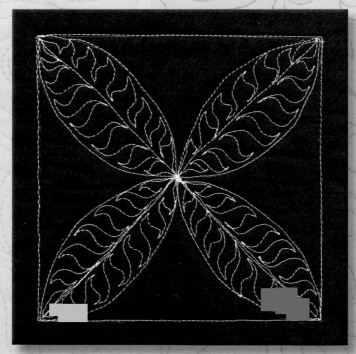

 American Quilter's Society

P. O. Box 3290 • Paducah, KY 42002-3290

www.AmericanQuilter.com

Located in Paducah, Kentucky, the American Quilter's Society (AQS) is dedicated to promoting the accomplishments of today's quilters. Through its publications and events, AQS strives to honor today's quiltmakers and their work and to inspire future creativity and innovation in quiltmaking.

Editor: Helen Squire
Technical Editor: Cheryl Barnes
Graphic Design: Lynda Smith
Cover Design: Michael Buckingham
Photography: Charles Lynch

Published by American Quilter's Society
in cooperation with Golden Threads.

Library of Congress Cataloging-in-Publication Data
Patten, Sue.
    Quilting possibilities : freehand filler patterns / by Sue Patten.
        p. cm.
    Summary: "Freehand quilting ideas and possibilities in three dozen traditional pieced blocks and worksheets that identify areas needing quilting. Additional filler patterns for cornerstones, sashing strips, and background quilting provided"-- Provided by publisher.
    ISBN 1-57432-918-9
    1. Patchwork--Patterns. 2. Quilting--Patterns. I. American Quilter's Society. II. Title.

TT835.P3856 2006
746.46'041--dc22

                        2006023486

Additional copies of this book may be ordered from the American Quilter's Society, PO Box 3290, Paducah, KY 42002-3290, or online at www.AmericanQuilter.com.

Dedication

The dedication for this book goes to my three children, Jessie, Micheal, and Alexis. Every path I take in life is meant to make their world a better place.

Acknowledgments

I would also like to include a special thanks to the incredible people who have guided me along the way: To my mom, Virginia, who nurtures and cares for my children when I am on the road. To Jill Pettit, who encouraged me to fly to Houston and introduced me to all the right people. To Linda Taylor, who once told me that my quilting should reflect who I am inside. To Marcia Stevens, whose support over the years has helped me every step of the way. To Cheryl Barnes, who believed in me enough to publish my patterns and make my design ideas come to life. To the entire Simon's Family of Quilters Rule, who make me feel like I am with family and not just friends when I am so far from home. To Jim Langland, Bob Ketcham, and Jim Kaldenberg, for their endless encouragement and support. I truly believe that the people in our lives help shape who we are and what we've become. I feel blessed to have had these people guiding me along the way.

Contents

Introduction 4

A Note to Readers 5

Sue's Tips and Tricks 6–8

Design Placement Suggestions 9–14
   Single Spine 9
   Single Spine with Inside Fillers 10
   Double Spine 11
   Double Spine with Fillers 12
   Floating Patterns 13
   Background Fillers 14

Freehand Fillers 15–19

Quilt as Inspired 20–93
   Joseph's Coat 20
   Four-Patch 22
   Nine-Patch 26
   Snowball 28
   Carrie Nation 30
   Letter H 32
   Indian Puzzle 34
   Card Trick 36
   Road to California 38
   Broken Wheel 40
   Mosaic No. 21 42
   Four X Variation 44
   Kansas Star 46

   Black-Eyed Susan 48
   Sashings & Cornerstones 49
   Orange Peel Variation 50
   Mosaic No. 17 52
   Double X No. 2 54
   Hovering Hawks 56
   Dutchman's Puzzle 58
   Whirligig 60
   Chinese Lantern 62
   Lady of the Lake 64
   The Windmill 66
   Log Cabin 68
   Square in a Square 70
   Around the World 72
   3 Petal Dresden Fan 74
   Double Pinwheel Whirls 76
   Sashings & Cornerstones 77
   6 Petal Dresden Fan 78
   Meadow Flowers 80
   Wheel of Fortune 82
   Dove in the Window 84
   Star of the East 86
   Optical Illusions 88
   Grist Mill 90
   Blazing Star 92
   Heart Flower II 94

About the Author 95

Introduction

As quilters, we spend weeks, months, even years creating the masterpieces we call quilt tops. We collect the perfect fabrics and follow the pattern instructions step-by-step. If by chance our seams turn out less than perfect, we remove the imperfect stitches and try again until the top is finished and we are happy with the end result. When we read through the pages of instructions to see what comes next, we find only three little words to help us—"quilt as desired." This is when most of us simply fold away our works of art and place them on a shelf in the closet, or stack them neatly with the rest of our finished tops in the corner of our sewing rooms.

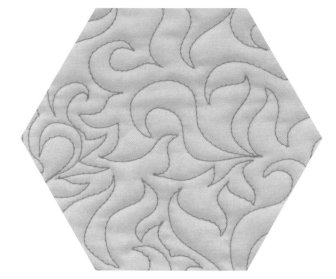

Of course we know that one day great inspiration will come to us and we will return to that quilt to complete it with as much excitement as we had the day we started piecing it. My hope is that today is that day.

I chose 36 different blocks from The Electric Quilt® Company design software (ww.electricquilt.com) and numbered them by the degree of difficulty for the quiltmaker. Next, I used my four favorite styles of freehand quilting: swirls, flames, feathers, and spheres to fill in the blocks (see examples on page 20–21.) Thirty interchangeable sashing and cornerstone designs were also sprinkled throughout the pieced or appliquéd blocks.

This book is filled with stitching designs to finish your unfinished works of art. Whether you quilt by hand, machine, or longarm, this book is meant to fill your mind with ideas that will help you "quilt as inspired" with three-dozen quilt blocks done in four different designs to inspire you.

I Remain Crazy For Longarm Quilting...

Sue Patten

A Note to Readers

Most quilters are strictly visual. Most people never take the time to read through the general instruction pages in any book. For them, a picture is worth a thousand pages of instructions and the rules of quilting are merely "suggestions." So for those of you taking the time to read this, I have a few extra tips, thoughts, and comments.

✳ Don't be afraid to use variegated thread. It adds extra color, a touch of flair, movement, or intense texture. Often, the changing colors of rainbows can take an average, well-pieced top from ordinary to spectacular.

✳ Choose a brightly colored thread for your main design and then match your filler thread with the background fabric. Most important of all, relax and let your creativity complete your work of art.

✳ Select your batting to fit the "look" you are hoping to achieve. High loft looks great if you plan to have areas in your quilt POP! Choose a low loft batting if the entire quilt will be heavily stitched.

✳ Whenever possible, figure a way to have your stitching patterns be continuous. Use the corners and/or seamlines of your patchwork to sneak through to the next shape. When I'm on a roll, I hate to stop and start.

✳ A heavily patterned backing fabric needs little to no attention, but also fails to show off your hours of quilting. Be brave and choose a solid color for the back of your masterpiece. With the right attention to detail, the end result is like a wholecloth of colorful thread designs. It's like having completed two quilts instead of one!

✳ I believe a quilt should be a reflection of the quilter, so let your heart do the stitching even if it means "breaking the rules."

Sue's Tips and Tricks

Free-motion quilting is meant to be an expression of the quilter. It does not have to be perfect; instead it should be "consistently inconsistent." I recommend starting with the spine or stem of the design, moving to a continuous design that follows the movement of the spine, and then, if need be, completing the pattern with an inside filler or background filler that complements the project.

✳ *If you hate to stitch in the ditch, just be sure that your designs touch the ditch often to keep it flat.*

✳ *Remember—any design that you can create large can also be done very small to create a stippled effect. Feathers, vines, and scribble stippling are so overdone nowadays. Spice it up with your own creation!*

All quilted samples made by the author

page 35 Touch the Ditch

page 38 Stippled Effect

page *45* Alter the Direction

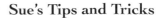

Shown here are only a few illustrated examples from the over 100 sketches in the book where I offer "suggestions" for quilting 36 different pieced blocks. My tips and tricks are highlighted—but remember, it's your quilt, so the only rules you have to follow are the ones you make up along the way.

✳ *To create extra movement. I will alter the direction of a design. Wherever possible, I like the light areas to flow clockwise and the design in the dark areas to run counter-clockwise.*

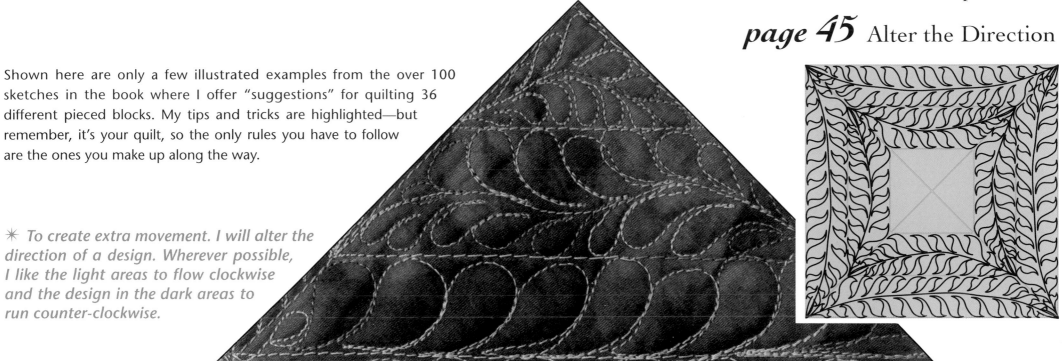

page *46*

Flip the Design

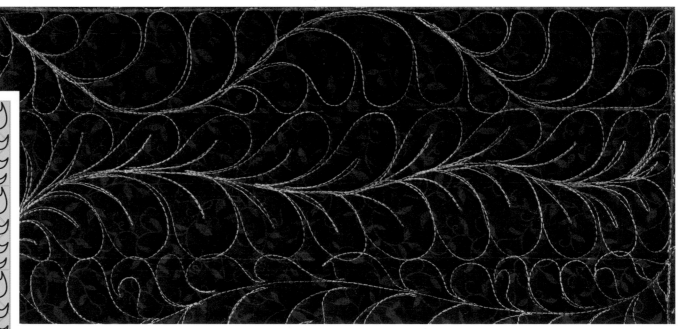

✳ *When using the same motif, I flip the design to create extra texture and movement.*

✳ *Mix pointed-edge designs such as vines with soft rounded designs such as feathers.*

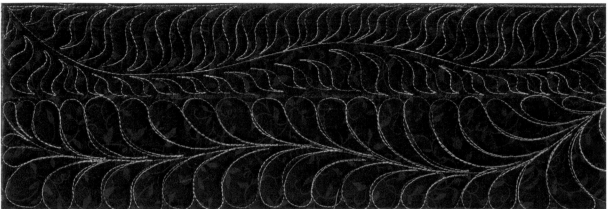

page 78
Mixed Shapes

page 83
Create a New Design

✳ *Whenever possible sneak through the corner to the next space. When not possible, find a line to travel—just be sure to enclose the area you are traveling around.*

page 85
Sneak Through the Corners

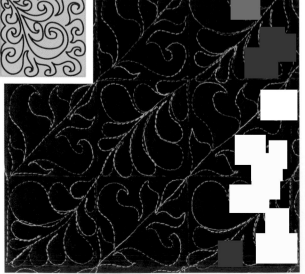

✳ *Your design does not have to be placed in every shape within your block. Often I create a design that travels through more than one shape and connect them to create an entirely new design within the block.*

Single Spine

The "spine" or "stem" is the line that moves through the center of the design. It is your starting point for all the designs shown throughout this book. A "single spine" design always starts and ends at a corner or on an outside edge.

When you reach the end of your spine, it is time to "hit your mark." This is the outer edge of the shape you are working in.

It is always better to be a little more on the inside of your shape than to have even a single stitch hit outside the shape.

The goal is to hit the ditch with a few stitches each time. To avoid having to stitch in the ditch, work your way back down the spine with the design and follow the spine back up the other side until the spine is enclosed.

If you find it easier to work in only one direction, then simply sneak back up or down your spine to complete the second side of the design.

Design Placement Suggestions

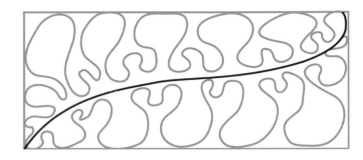

Hit Your Mark refers to stitching to the outer edges of the shape or area to be quilted.

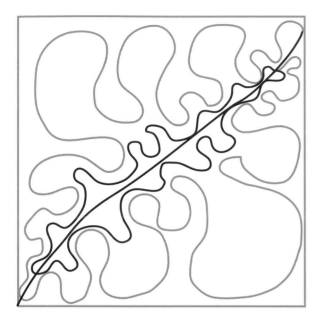

Single Spine with Inside Fillers

With this method of quilting, your filler will be on the inside of the design. I only use an "inside filler" when the shape I am working on is very large and requires more stitches to secure the area.

A filler should complement your design but not be overpowering. It can be as simple as echo quilting inside your "hit the mark" design or as complex as creating a completely new design to fill the empty space.

The filler starts as soon as you reach the end of hitting your mark. I do not cast off or end my threads—I simply go from the finishing point of the outer stitches and sneak back inside the design via the spine.

Double Spine

For a more intense custom finish, I recommend a "double spine" design. This simply means that you will be stitching two spine designs in the same shape. I suggest curving both spines towards opposite outside edges and filling in your "hit the mark" on both spines before filling in the center.

I like to leave a scant one-half inch empty between the inside designs. Also, it looks better when the spines only touch in the bottom corners of the shape—leaving the top of the design slightly open.

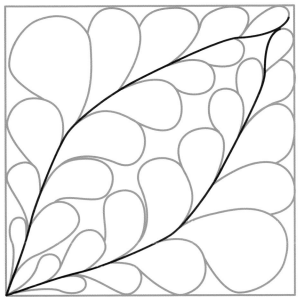

Double Spine with Fillers

To spice things up and add extra texture and depth to your shape, try using a creative inside filler. The inside design should complement the "hit the mark" design but can be more or less intense then the outer design.

For these designs, I like my spines to enclose the center and still be as close to the corners as possible. Ideally, they should touch the corners so they can be used to sneak through the corner via the spine to the next shape.

Floating Patterns

You also have the choice of "floating" your main design inside the shape. In this method, the spine does not hit any outside edges or corners.

Stitch your spine at least one inch in from the edge of the shape or place a swirling circle inside the shape.

To complete this design, continue your pattern around the spine NOT hitting the ditch and having both ends of the spine enclosed. I suggest flipping the direction of your design in the center of the spine to create a mirror image. If needed, your "filler" will be on the outside of your design. (Refer to page 14.)

Background Fillers

There are as many background fillers as there are designs. Choose one that complements your quilt and that you are comfortable with and go for it. It can be as simple as "echo quilting" or as intense as "micro-stippling."

Whichever design method you use—inside or outside the shape—the end result should be a reflection of not only the patchwork design, but of you, the quilter.

Freehand Fillers

QUESTIONABLE BLOOMS

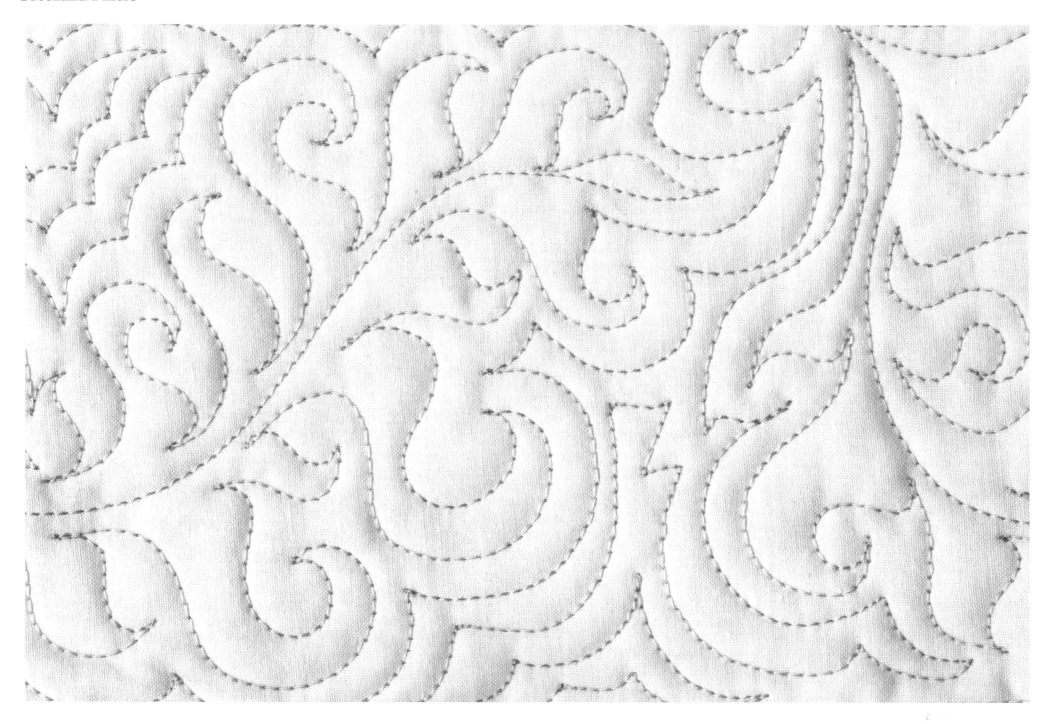

FLOATING FERNS

FEATHERS & FERNS

QUESTIONABLE QUESTION MARKS

DANCING FLAMES

Quilt As Inspired

SPHERES

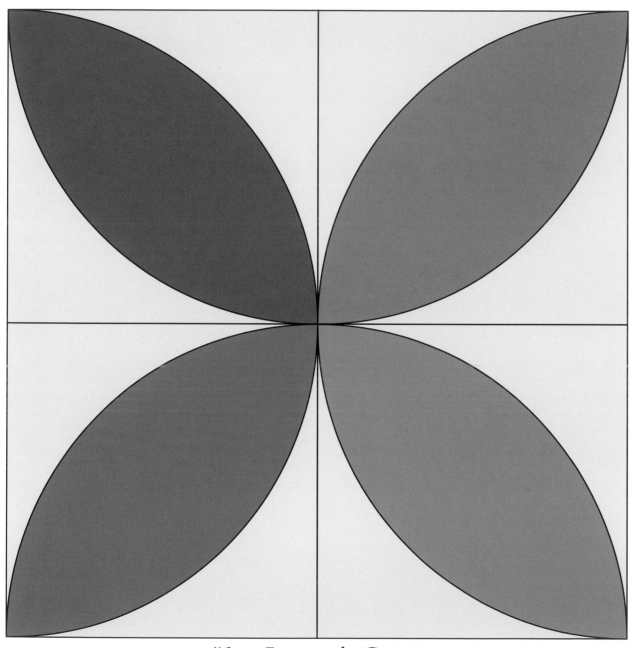

#1 – JOSEPH'S COAT

FLAMES

FEATHERS

SWIRLS

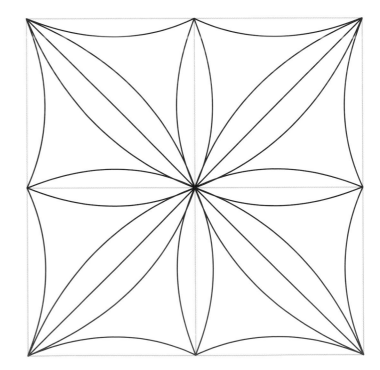

#2 – FOUR-PATCH

#2 – FOUR-PATCH

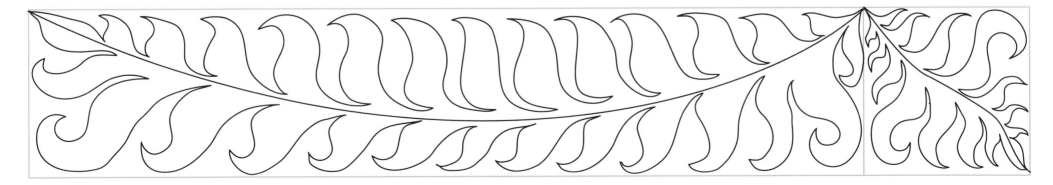

#3 – NINE-PATCH

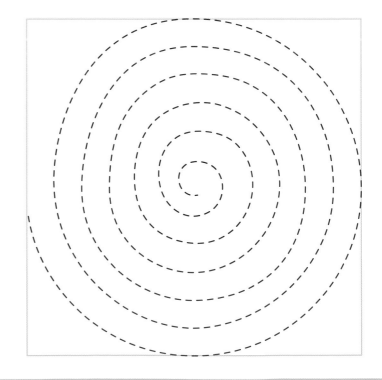

#4 – SNOWBALL

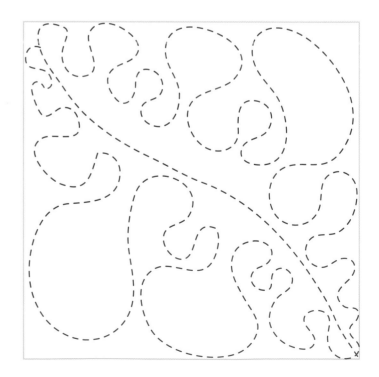

#5 – CARRIE NATION

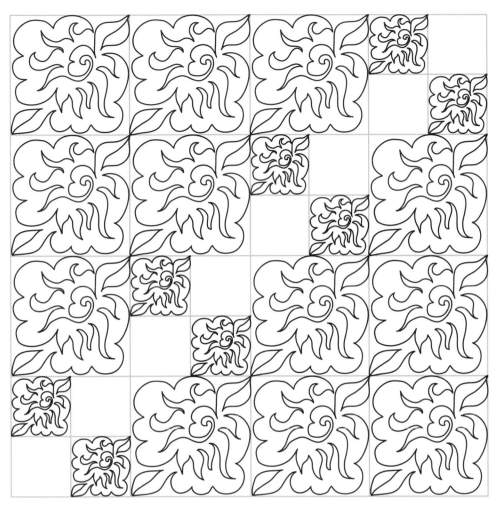

Brainless Resizing

"Freehand filler patterns" is really an oxymoron. My designs are ideas, *NOT* patterns to be followed diligently. However, changing the size of a quilting design (as shown above, and on page 39) will add extra interest and dimension within the quilt and having a visual reference to look at helps when planning the overall quilting.

Used as guidelines only, you have my written permission to make extra copies and to use a scanner or copier to enlarge or reduce a design to fit a specific space.

I recommend the Quilter's Assistant Proportional Scale (QAPRO) by Golden Threads®, available at local quilt, fabric, and craft shops, or order direct: www.goldenthreads.com.

This handy tool takes the math out of resizing as you simply dial the size of "what you have" to "what you want," line up the numbers, and look in the opening for the percentage of change!

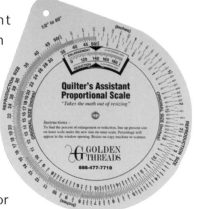

#6 – LETTER H

#7 – INDIAN PUZZLE

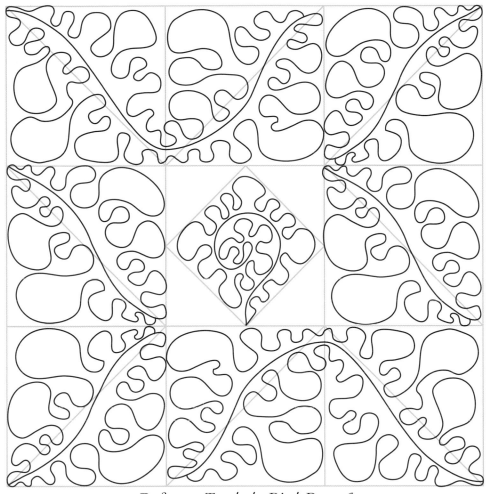

Refer to *Touch the Ditch* Page 6

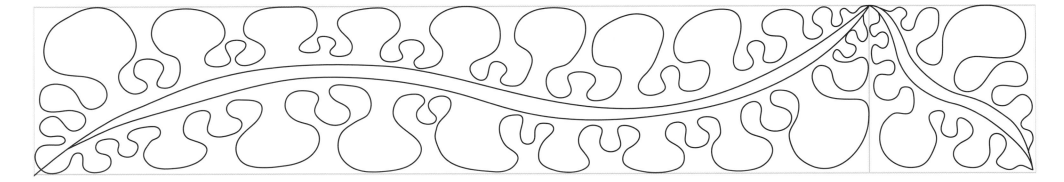

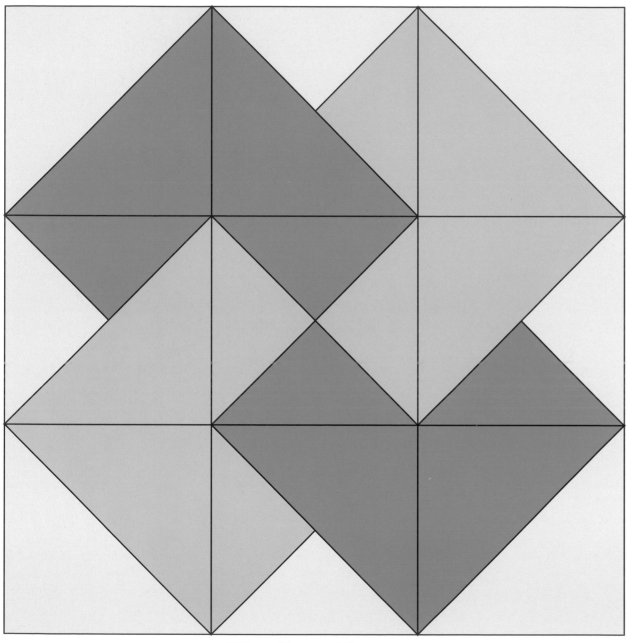

#8 – Card Trick

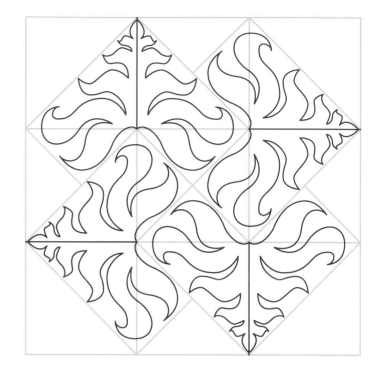

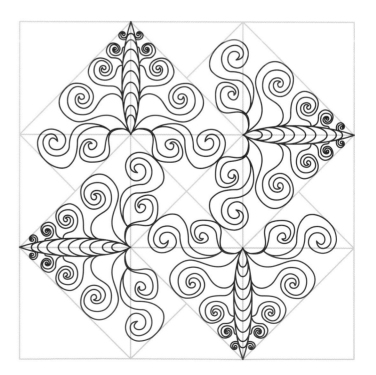

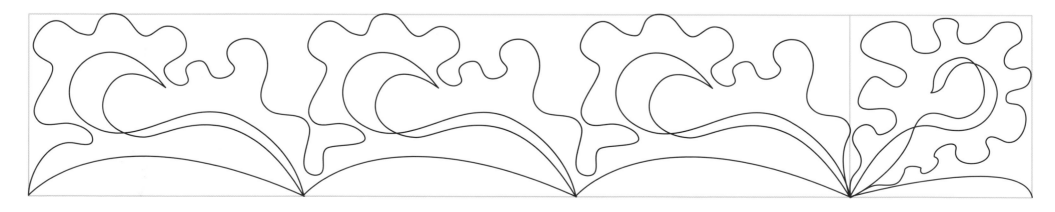

Refer to *Stippled Effect*, page 6

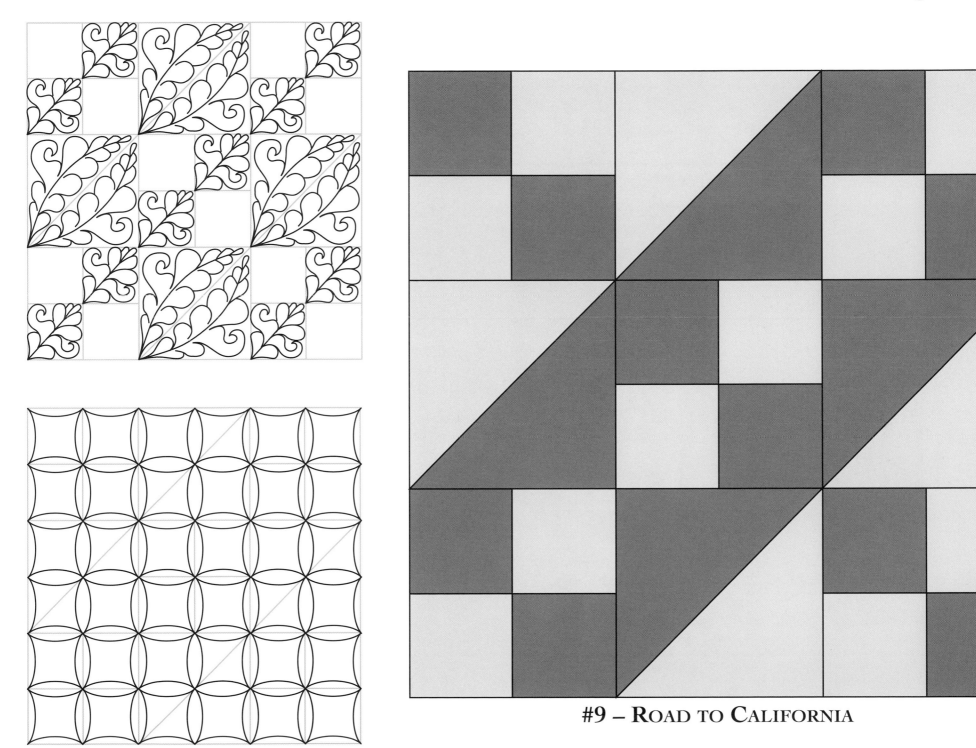

#9 – ROAD TO CALIFORNIA

#10 – BROKEN WHEEL

#11 – MOSAIC NO. 21

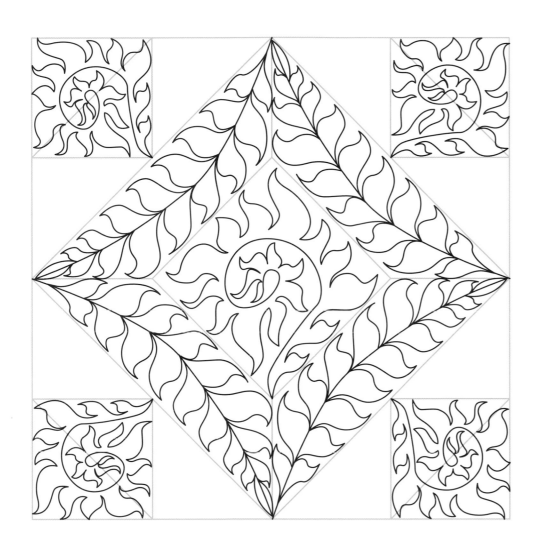

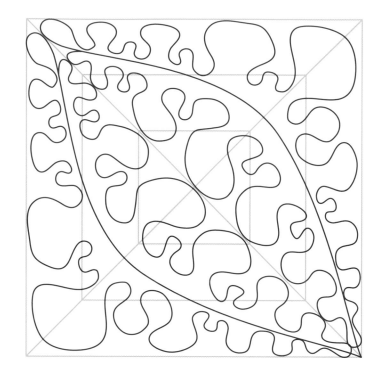

12 – FOUR X VARIATION

Refer to *Alter the Direction*, page 7

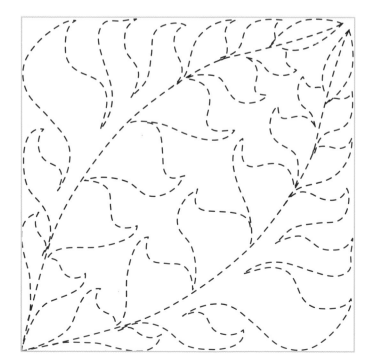

Refer to *Flip the Design,* page 7

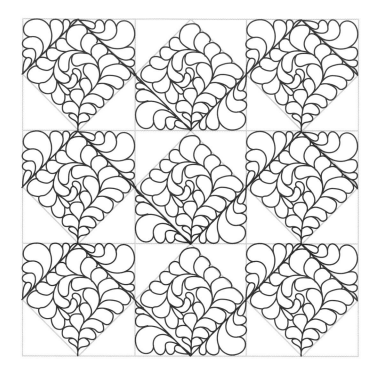

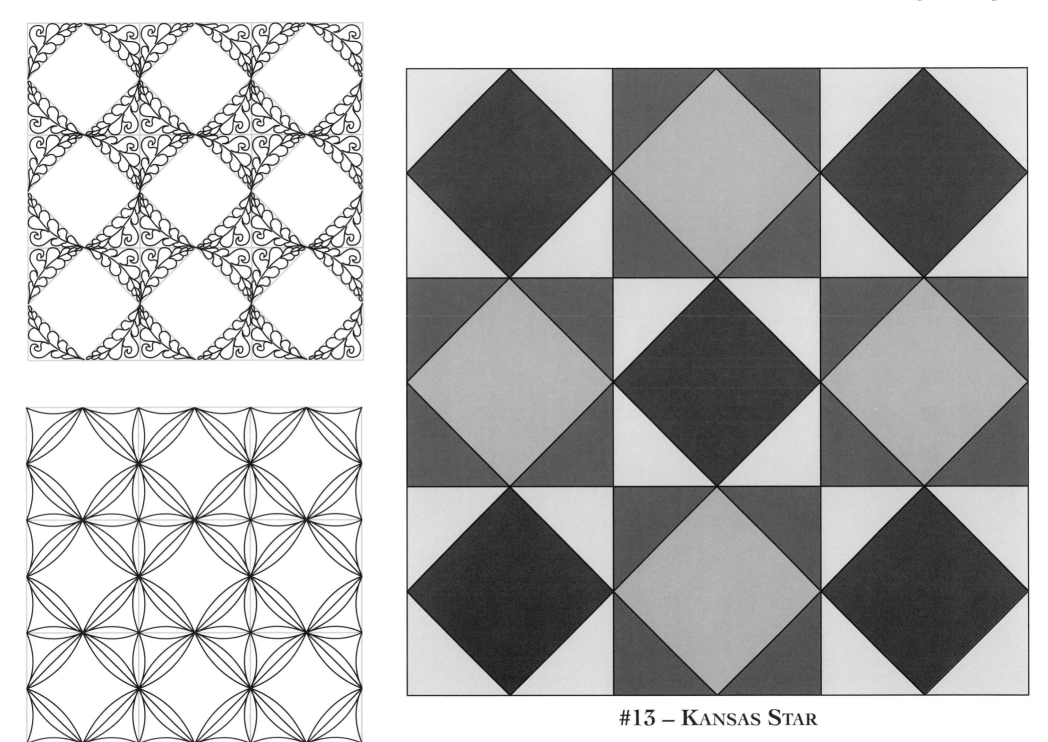

#13 – KANSAS STAR

#14 – BLACK-EYED SUSAN

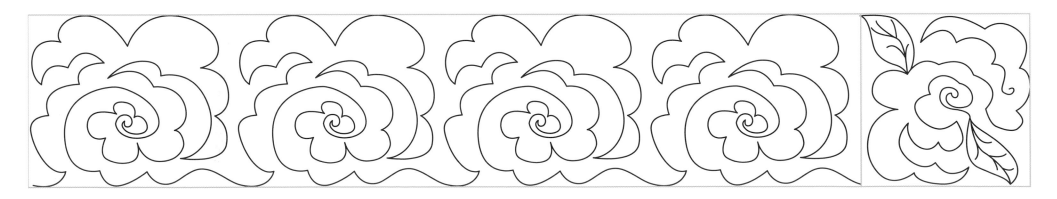

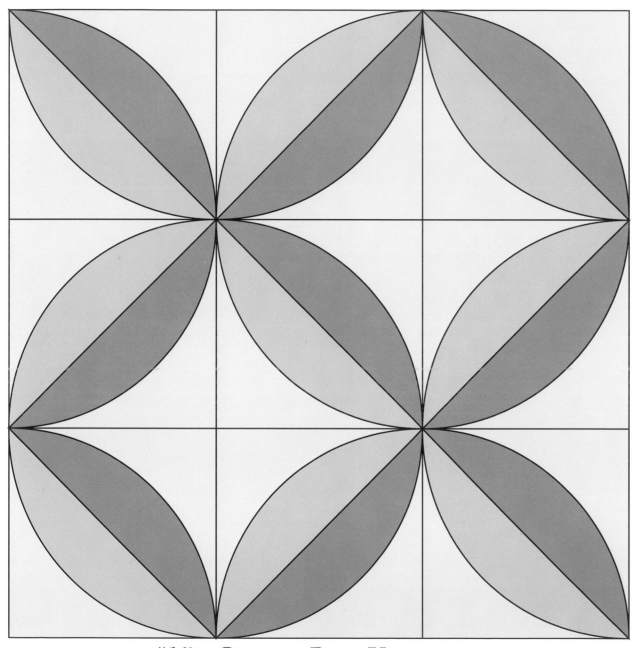

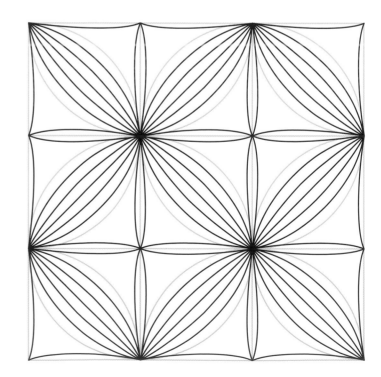

#15 – ORANGE PEEL VARIATION

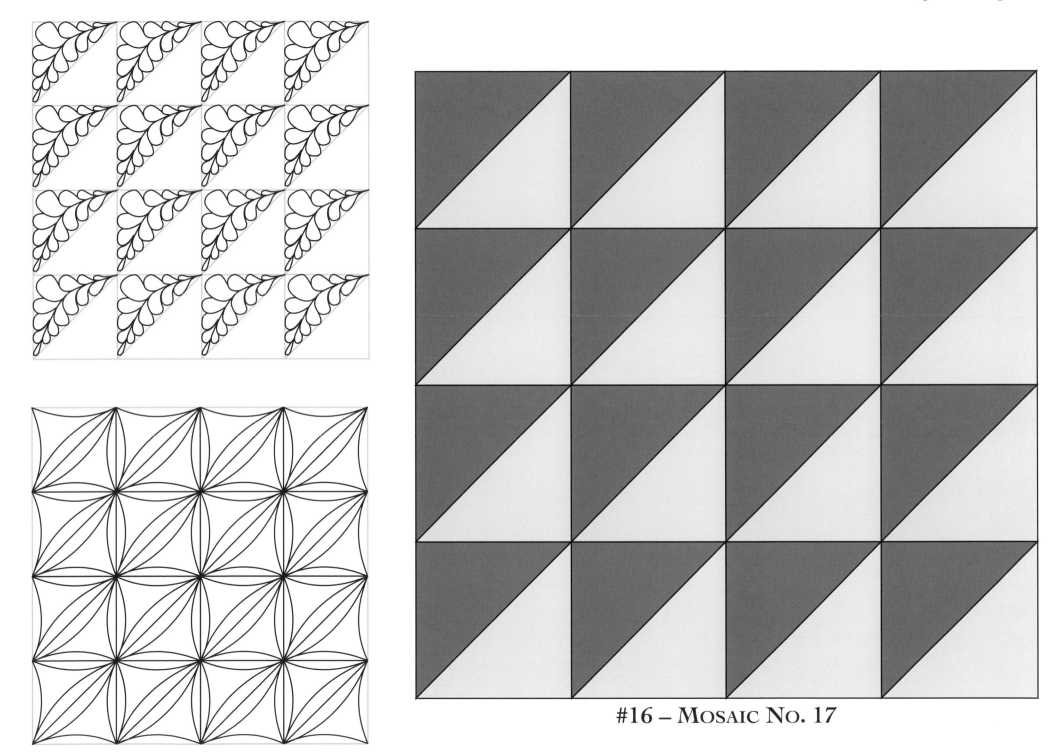

#16 – MOSAIC NO. 17

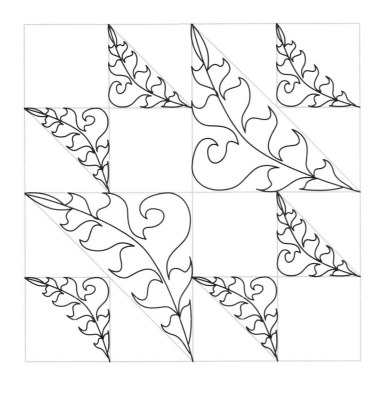

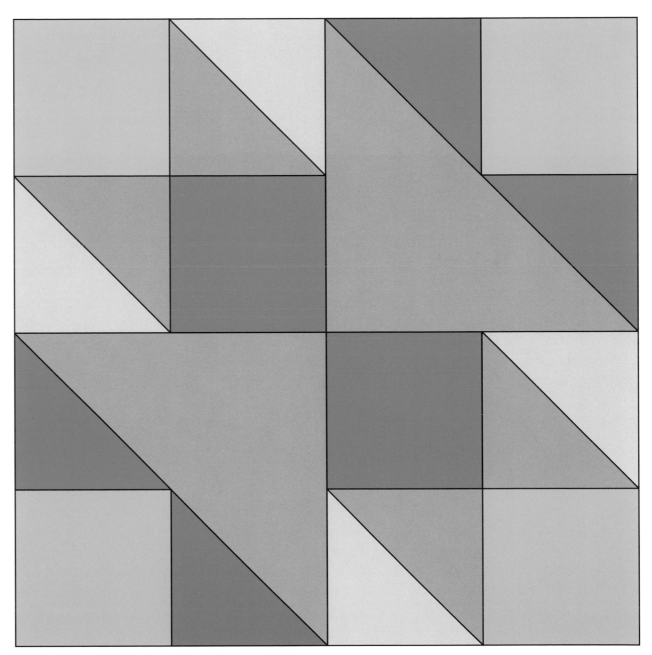

#17 – DOUBLE X NO. 2

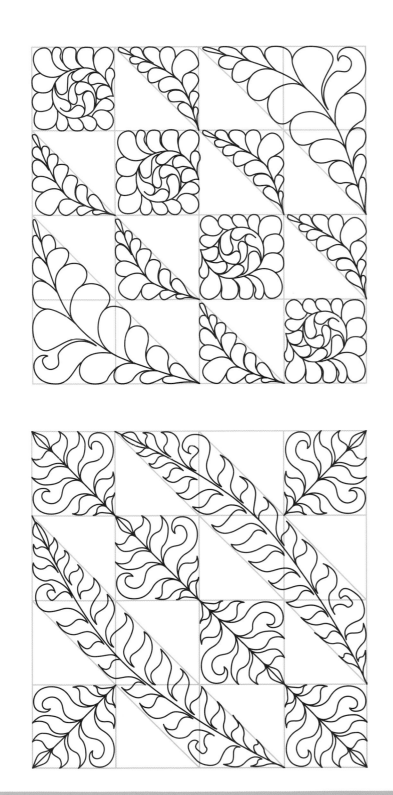

#18 – HOVERING HAWKS

#19– DUTCHMAN'S PUZZLE

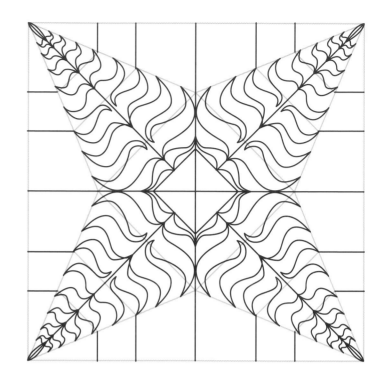

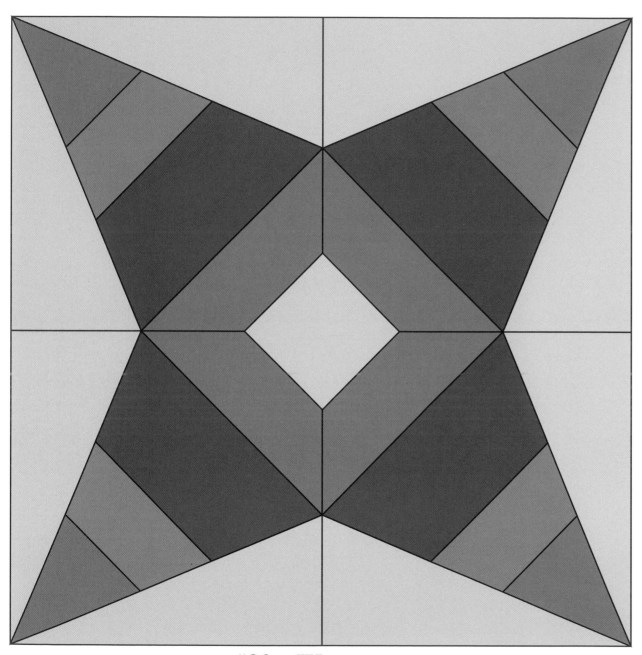

#20 – WHIRLIGIG

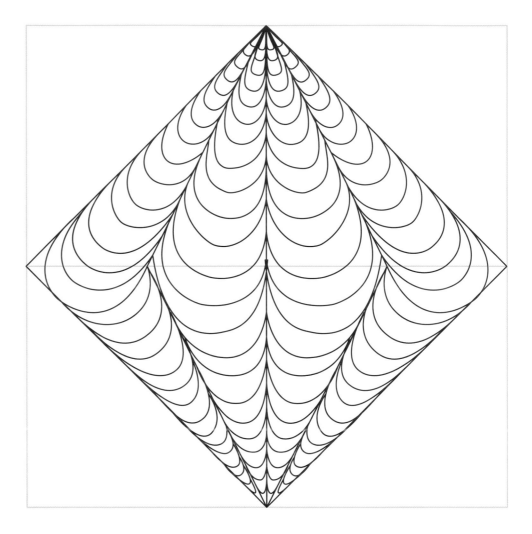

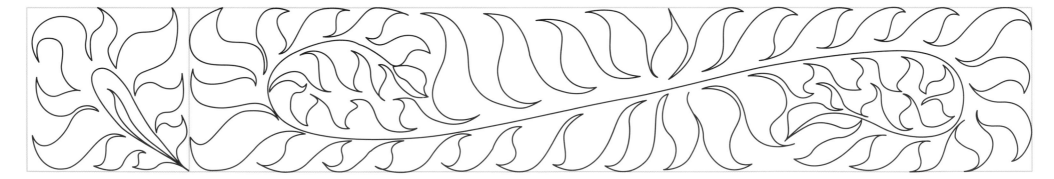

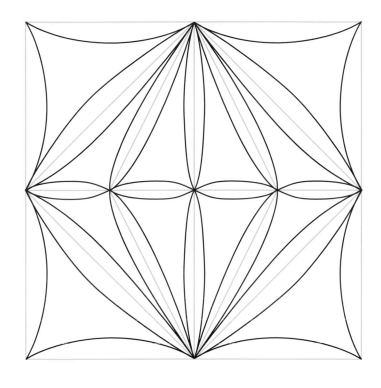

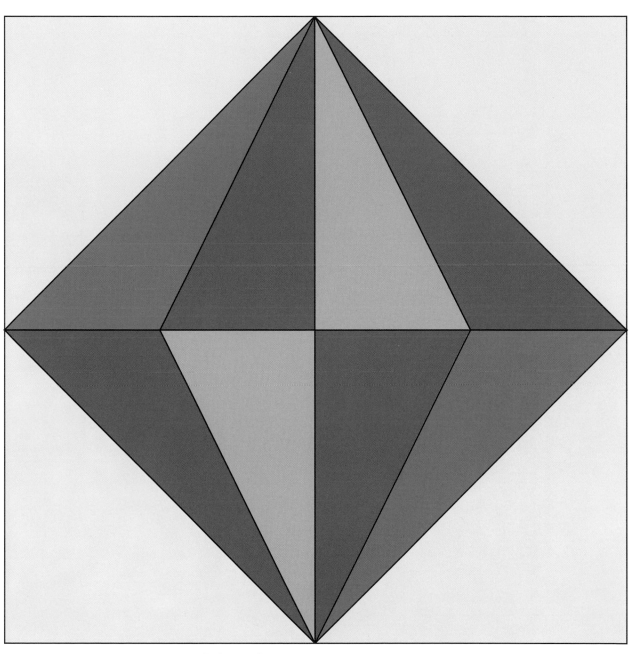

#21 – CHINESE LANTERNS

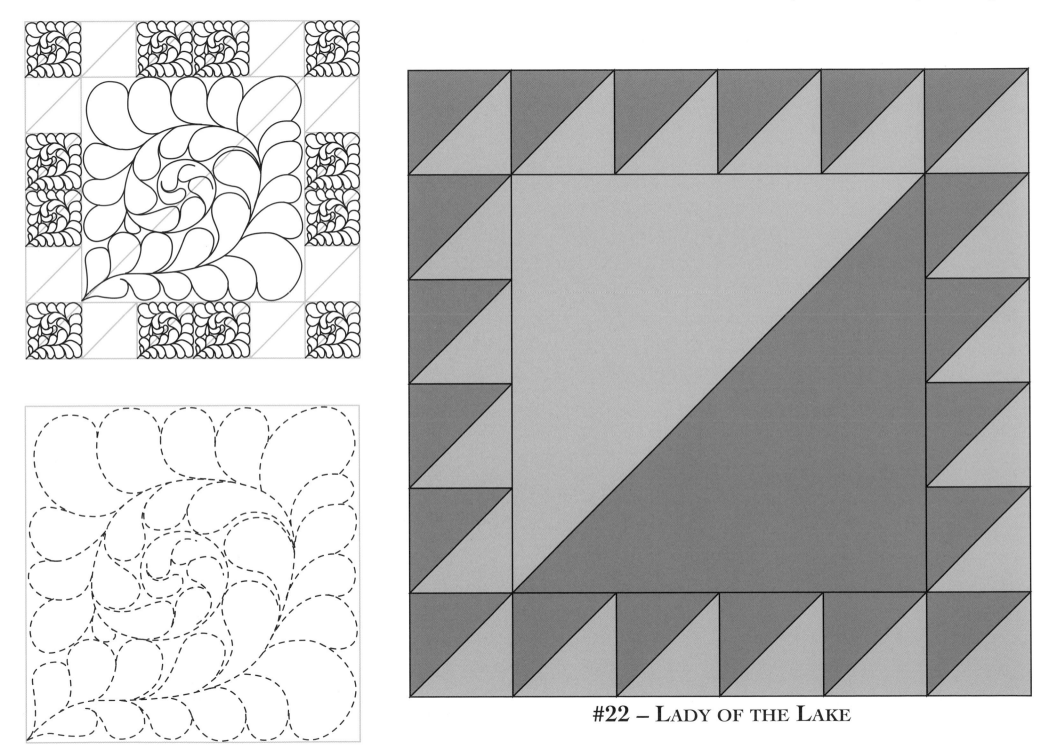

#22 – LADY OF THE LAKE

#23 – WINDMILL

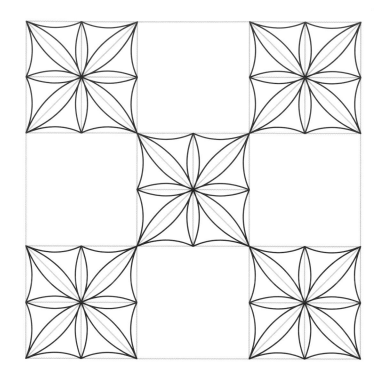

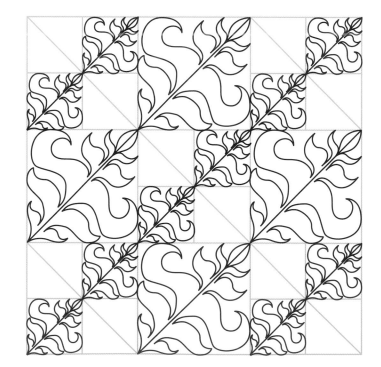

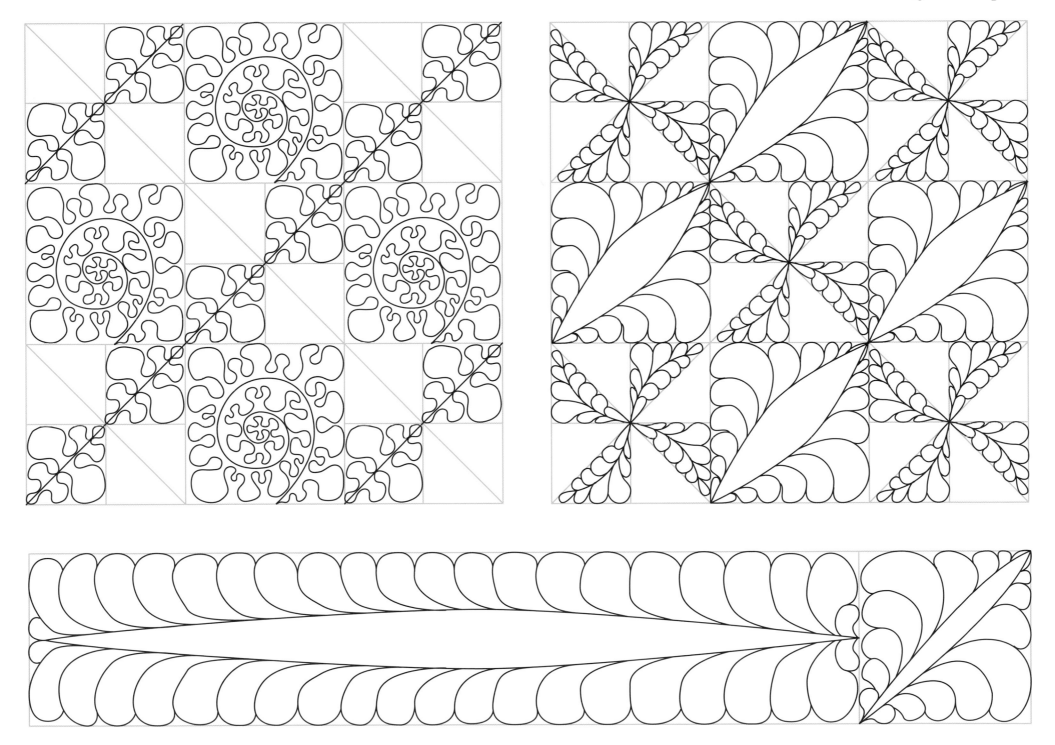

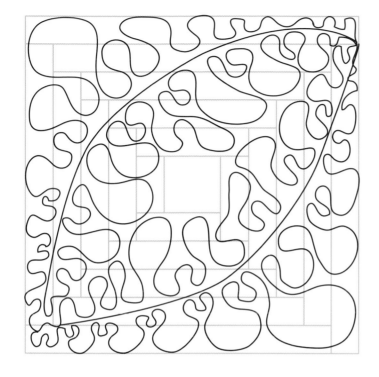

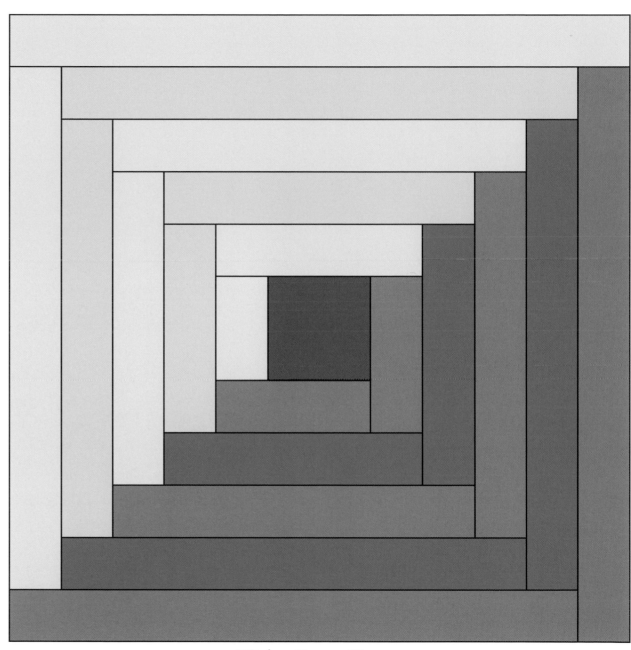

#24 – Log Cabin

#25 – SQUARE IN A SQUARE

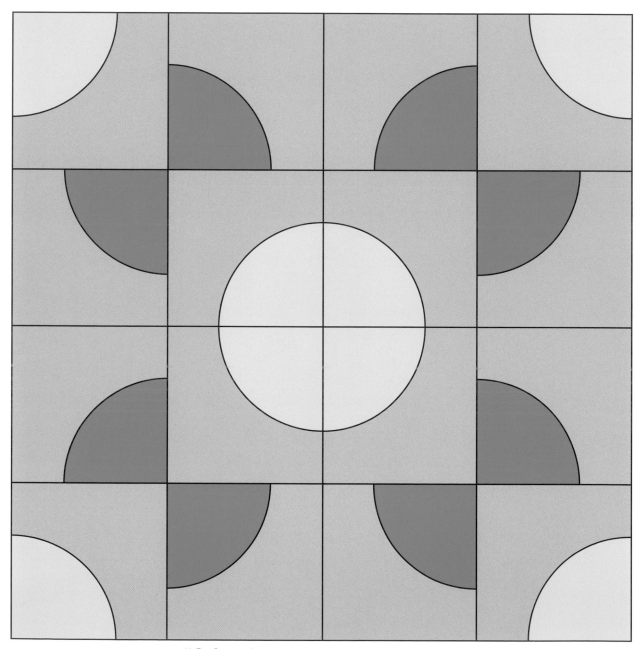

#26 – AROUND THE WORLD

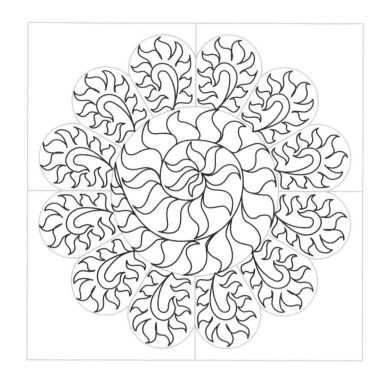

#27 – 3 Petal Dresden Fan

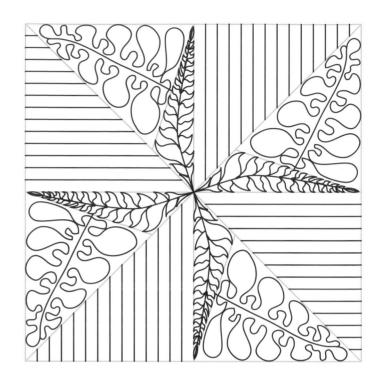

#28 – PINWHEEL

Refer to *Mixed Shapes,* page 8

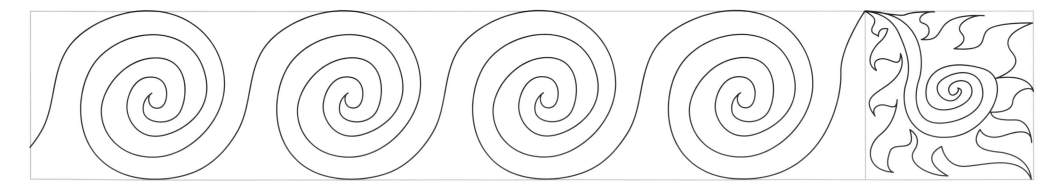

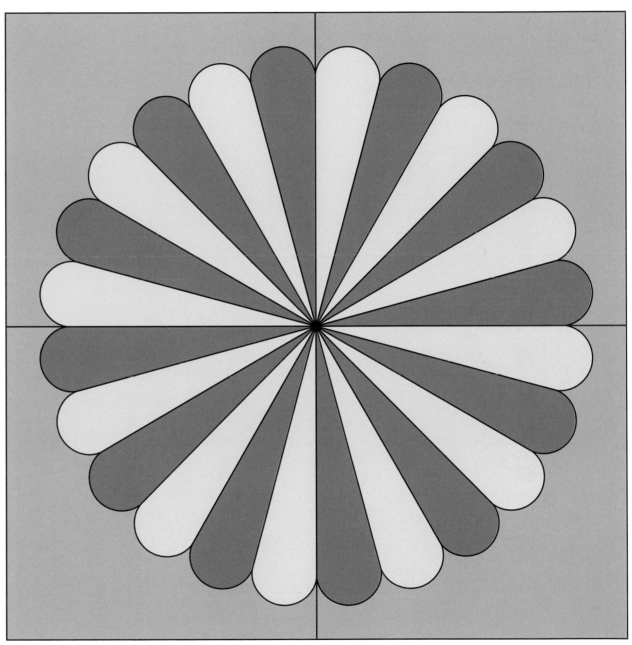

#29 – 6 PETAL DRESDEN FAN

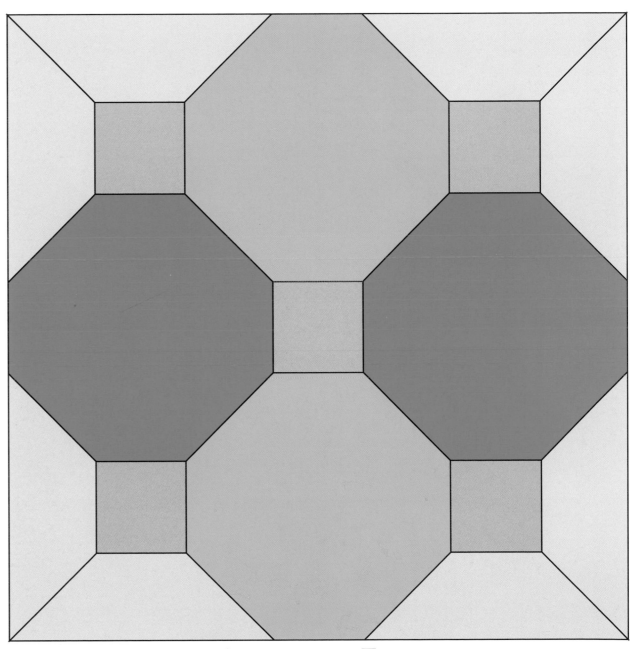

#30 – MEADOW FLOWER

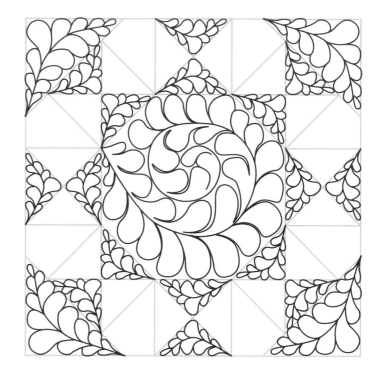

#31 – WHEEL OF FORTUNE

Refer to *Create a New Design*, page 8

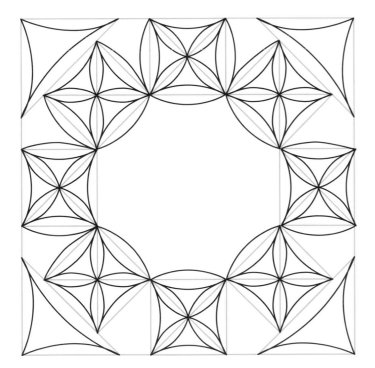

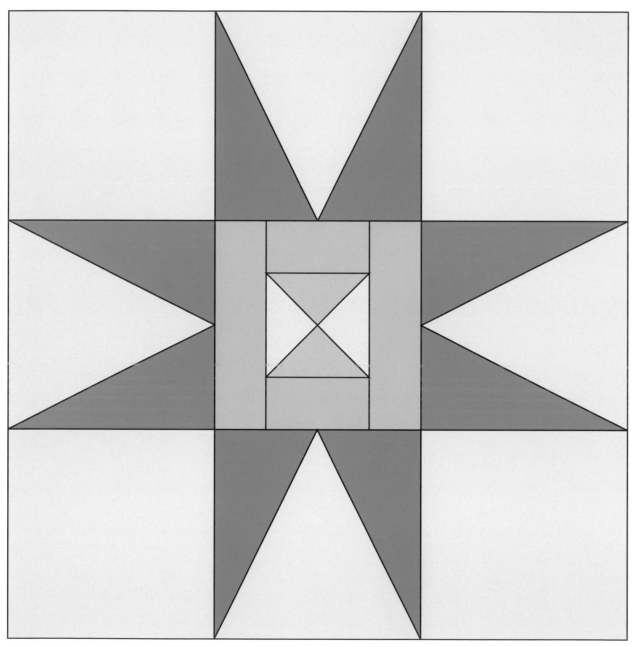

#32 – DOVE IN THE WINDOW

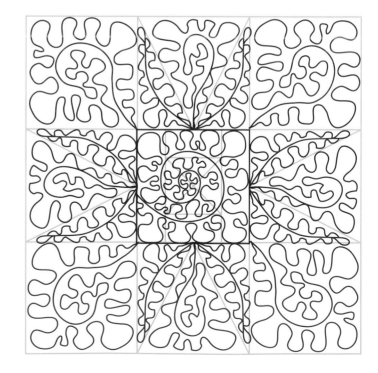

Refer to *Sneak Through the Corners*, page 8

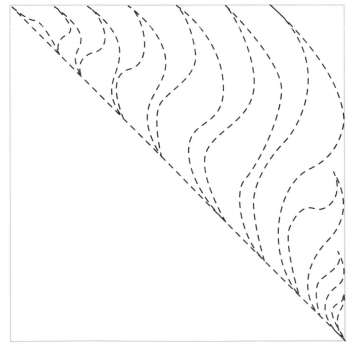

#33 – STAR OF THE EAST

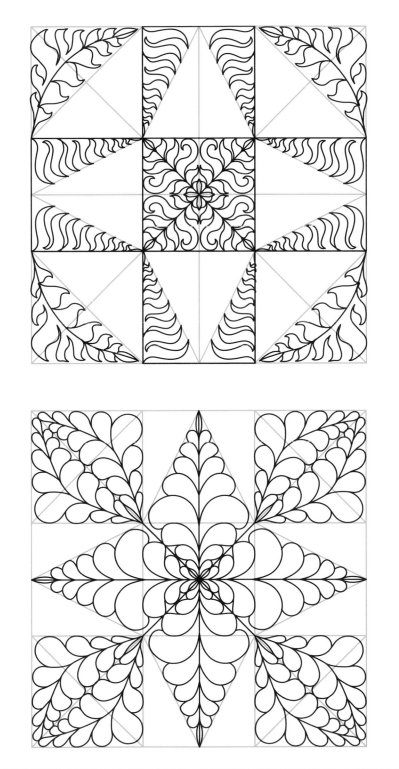

#34 – OPTICAL ILLUSION

#35 – GRIST MILL

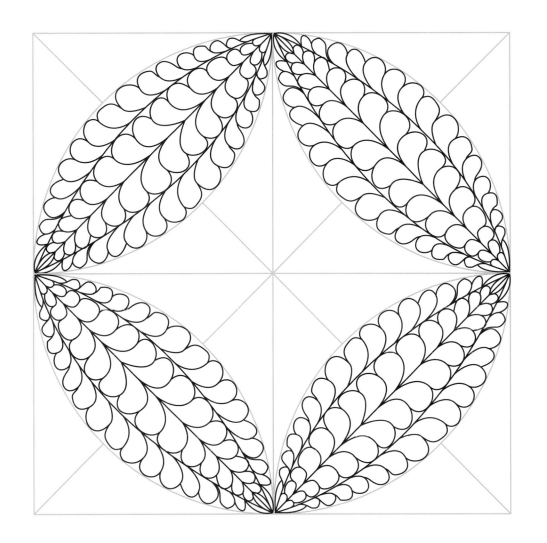

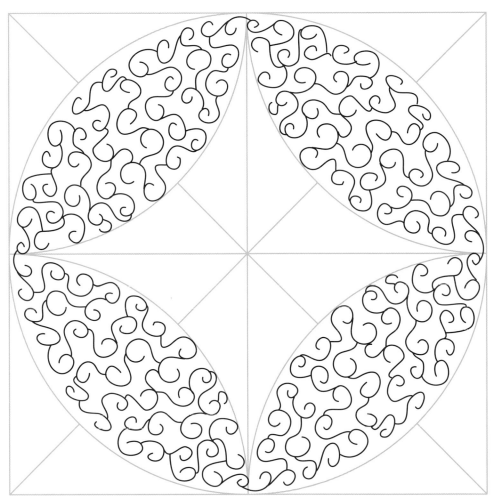

#36 – BLAZING STAR

Quilt as Inspired

#37 – HEART FLOWER II

QUILTING POSSIBILITIES... Freehand Filler Patterns – Sue Patten

About the Author

Sue Patten has been blazing her own trail through the quilting industry since she began piecing quilts and hand quilting in 1991. As her quilting style evolved, she plunged into machine quilting in 2000. As with every new challenge Sue faces, she embarked on her machine quilting journey with her natural energy and a hearty appetite for knowledge.

Now several years down the road, Sue has taken machine quilting to a new level and developed an edgy style that is totally unique to her. Along this voyage she discovered a new sense of fulfillment through teaching her techniques to other machine quilters. Sue now works out of her own longarm training studio in Hagersville, Ontario, Canada, where she teaches a wide range of classes to quilters on every level from beginners to more advanced. She also enjoys teaching specialty classes showcasing more innovative techniques that she is passionate about, such as "Cut Away," snippets techniques, and thread art. Not only does she teach in her own studio, but Sue is always on the move! She frequently travels throughout Canada, the United States, and Europe to educate others in the art of longarm machine quilting.

Throughout her quilting career, Sue has been featured on *Linda's Longarm Quilting* with Linda Taylor and her quilts have appeared on *Sue Warden CraftScapes*. Her quilt artistry has also been featured in various books and magazines, such as *Better Homes & Gardens*, *Dream Catcher*, Rosemary Makhan's *Biblical Blocks*, and Virginia A. Walton's *Slow Down, Curves Ahead*.

In the scant spare time she has, Sue also enjoys designing edge-to-edge pattern packs, embroidery, and thread art by numbers kits. Some of her most creative and innovative patterns are published and marketed by Golden Threads in the United States. As time allows, she also designs and teaches at her local quilt shop, Quilter's Dream.

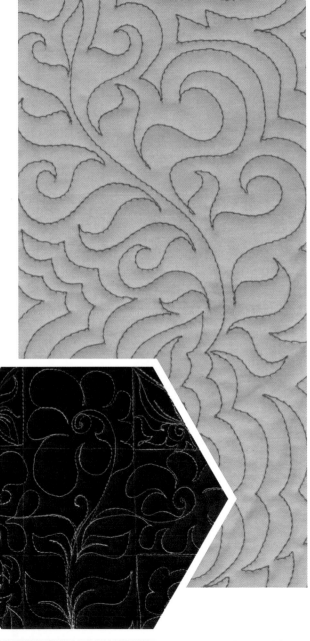

On a more personal note, Sue's most rewarding role by far is that of single parent to three delightful children. Her deepest passion is, of course, spending time with Jessica, Micheal, and Alexis. The children have their own creative interests, and Sue thrives on their artistic energy and draws inspiration for many of her projects from working with her kids.

Other AQS Books

This is only a small selection of the books available from the American Quilter's Society. AQS books are known worldwide for timely topics, clear writing, beautiful color photos, and for accurate illustrations and patterns. The following books are available from your local bookseller or quilt shop.

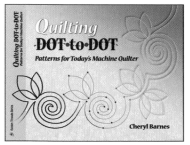

Quilting DOT-to-DOT
Patterns for Today's Machine Quilter
Cheryl Barnes
#6900   12" x 9" us$24.95

The Best of Shirley Thompson QUILTING PATTERNS
Compiled by Cheryl Barnes
#6571   12" x 9" us$24.95

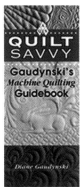

QUILT SAVVY
Gaudynski's Machine Quilting Guidebook
Diane Gaudynski
#6898   us$21.95

CREATE AND PRINT WITH Helen Squire
750 CD-ROM
Hand & Machine Quilting
#6288   us$29.95

Helen's Mix & Match QUILTING PATTERNS
Helen Squire
#6800   us$22.95

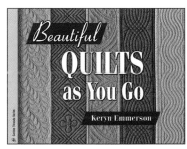

Beautiful QUILTS as You Go
Keryn Emmerson
#6803   12" x 9" us$22.95

Helen's Print & Use Quilting Patterns
HELEN SQUIRE
#6099   us$29.95

Infinite Feathers QUILTING PATTERNS to print with bonus patterns
Anita Shackelford
CD-ROM
#6521   us$29.95

THE ART OF Feather Quilting
Judy Allen
#6678   12" x 9" us$22.95

Pathways to Better Quilting
5 shapes for machine quilt patterns
SALLY TERRY
#6509   12" x 9" us$22.95

Look for these books nationally. **Call** or **Visit** our Web site at

1-800-626-5420
www.AmericanQuilter.com

GT Products

Companion Pattern Packs from Sue Patten!

Plumes
Quilt It with
by Sue Patten
#SP102 us$11.95

Swirls
Quilt It with
by Sue Patten
#SP104 us$11.95

Spheres
Quilt It with
by Sue Patten
#SP103 us$11.95

Flames
Quilt It with
by Sue Patten
#SP101 us$11.95

Continuous line quilting patterns for blocks, borders, corners or insets.

Available at quilt shops, fabric stores, quilting frame and sewing machine dealers, catalogs, or order direct.

GOLDEN THREADS
www.goldenthreads.com